The nation behaves well if it treats the natural resources as assets which it must turn over to the next generation increased; and not impaired in value.

Theodore Roosevelt

He who plants a tree. Plants a hope.

Lucy Larcom

Even if I knew that tomorrow the world would go to pieces, I would still plant my apple tree.

Martin Luther

You can't have the fruits without the roots.
Stephen Covey

Never say there is nothing beautiful in the world anymore. There is always something to make you wonder in the shape of a tree, the trembling of a leaf.

Albert Schweitzer

The clearest way into the Universe
is through a forest wilderness.

John Muir

If trees could scream, would we be so cavalier about
cutting them down? We might, if they screamed all
the time, for no good reason.

Jack Handey

Trees're always a relief, after people.

David Mitchell

It is difficult to realize how great a part of all that is cheerful and delightful in the recollections of our own life is associated with trees.

Wilson Flagg

A nation that destroys its soils destroys itself.
Forests are the lungs of our land, purifying the
air and giving fresh strength to our people.

Franklin D. Roosevelt

Between every two pine trees there is
a door leading to a new way of life.

John Muir

Alone with myself the trees bend to caress me the shade hugs my heart.

Candy Polgarr

Love is like a tree, it grows of its own accord, it puts down deep roots into our whole being.

Victor Hugo

Until you dig a hole, you plant a tree, you water it and make it survive, you haven't done a thing. You are just talking.

Wangari Maathai

I feel a great regard for trees;
they represent age and beauty and
the miracles of life and growth.

Louise Dickinson Rich

This oak tree and me, we're made of the same stuff.

Carl Sagan

There are more life forms in a handful of forest soil than there are people on the planet.

Peter Wohlleben

All our wisdom is stored in the trees.

Santosh Kalwar

Someone's sitting in the shade
today because someone planted
a tree a long time ago.

Warren Buffett

Until you dig a hole, you plant a tree, you water it and make it survive, you haven't done a thing. You are just talking

Wangari Maathai

Trees exhale for us so that we can inhale
them to stay alive. Can we ever forget that?
Let us love trees with every breath we take
until we perish.

Munia Khan

The true meaning of life is to plant trees,
under whose shade you do not expect to sit.

Nelson Henderson

Someone's sitting in the shade today because someone planted a tree a long time ago.

Warren Buffett

Trees are as close to immortality
as the rest of us ever come.

Karen Joy Fowler

You know me, I think there ought to be a big old tree right there. And let's give him a friend. Everybody needs a friend.

Bob Ross

Trees do not preach learning and precepts. They preach, undeterred by particulars, the ancient law of life.

Herman Hesse

The true meaning of life is to plant trees,
under whose shade you do not expect to sit.

Nelson Henderson

What we are doing to the forests of
the world is but a mirror reflection
of what we are doing to ourselves
and to one another.

Chris Maser

I feel a great regard for trees; they represent age
and beauty and the miracles of life and growth.

Louise Dickinson Rich

The creation of a thousand forests is in one acorn.

Ralph Waldo Emerson

Love the trees until their leaves fall off,
then encourage them to try again next year.

Chad Sugg

Whoever has learned how to listen to trees no longer wants to be a tree. He wants to be nothing except what he is. That is home. That is happiness.

Herman Hesse

The care of the Earth is our most
ancient and most worthy, and after
all, our most pleasing responsibility.

Wendell Berry

The best friend on earth of man is the tree.
When we use the tree respectfully and
economically, we have one of the greatest
resources on the earth.

Frank Lloyd Wright

The only thing that ultimately matters is to eat
an ice-cream cone, play a slide trombone, plant a
small tree, good God, now you're free.

Ray Manzarek

The best time to plant a tree was 20 years ago. The second best time is now.

Chinese Proverb

Trees exhale for us so that we can inhale them to stay alive. Can we ever forget that? Let us love trees with every breath we take until we perish.

Munia Khan

A tree is known by its fruit; a man by his deeds. A good deed is never lost; he who sows courtesy reaps friendship, and he who plants kindness gathers love.

Basil

When trees burn, they leave the smell
of heartbreak in the air.

Jodi Thomas

Trees are poems that the earth writes upon the sky.

Kahlil Gebran

On the last day of the world I would
want to plant a tree.

W.S. Merwin

Between every two pines is a
doorway to a new world.

John Muir

He that plants trees, loves others besides himself.
Thomas Fuller

Of all man's works of art, a cathedral is greatest. A vast and majestic tree is greater than that.

Henry Ward

What we are doing to the forests of the world is but a mirror reflection of what we are doing to ourselves and to one another.

Mahatma Gandhi

One touch of nature makes
the whole world kin.

William Shakespeare

The creation of a thousand forests is in one acorn.

Ralph Waldo Emerson

That each day I may walk unceasingly on the banks of my water, that my soul may repose on the branches of the trees which I planted, that I may refresh myself under the shadow of my sycamore.

Egyptian tomb inscription

To really feel a forest canopy one must use different senses, and often the most useful one is the sense of imagination.

Joan Maloof

Love the trees until their leaves fall off,
then encourage them to try again next year.

Chad Sugg

Trees are poems that the earth writes upon the sky.

Khalil Gibran

Listen to the trees as they sway in the wind. Their leaves are telling secrets. Their bark sings songs of olden days as it grows around the trunks. And their roots give names to all things. Their language has been lost. But not the gestures.

Vera Nazarian

All our wisdom is stored in the trees.

Santosh Kalwar

Whoever has learned how to listen to trees no longer wants to be a tree. He wants to be nothing except what he is. That is home. That is happiness.

Herman Hesse

Even if I knew that tomorrow the world would go to pieces, I would still plant my apple tree.

Martin Luther

Reversing deforestation is complicated;
planting a tree is simple.

Martin O'Malley

The care of the Earth is our most ancient and most worthy, and after all, our most pleasing responsibility.

Wendell Berry

Trees are poems that earth writes upon the sky, We fell them down and turn them into paper, That we may record our emptiness.

Khalil Gibran

A society grows great when old men plant trees whose shade they know they shall never sit in.

Greek Proverb

This solitary Tree! a living thing produced
too slowly ever to decay; of form and
aspect too magnificent to be destroyed.

William Wordsworth

I said to the almond tree,
'Friend, speak to me of
God,' and the almond tree
blossomed.

Nikos Kazantzakis

You know me, I think there ought to be a big old tree right there. And let's give him a friend. Everybody needs a friend.

Bob Ross

The tree which moves some to tears of joy is in the eyes of others only a green thing that stands in the way. Some see Nature all ridicule and deformity, and some scarce see Nature at all. But to the eyes of the man of imagination, Nature is Imagination itself..

William Blake

If a tree dies, plant another in its place.

Carolus Linnaeus

Trees are the best monuments that a man
can erect to his own memory. They speak
his praises without flattery, and they are
blessings to children yet unborn.

Lord Orrery

And see the peaceful trees extend their myriad
leaves in leisured dance-they bear the weight of
sky and cloud upon the fountain of their veins.

Kathleen Raine

We can learn a lot from trees: they're always grounded but never stop reaching heavenward.

Everett Mamor

Trees are sanctuaries. Whoever knows how to speak to them; whoever knows how to listen to them, can learn the truth. They do not preach learning and precepts, they preach undeterred by particulars, the ancient law of life.

Hermann Hesse

The only time I can really relax is up a tree
or somewhere outside. I love being outside.

Tom Felton

Of the infinite variety of fruits which spring from the bosom of the earth, the trees of the wood are the greatest in dignity.

Susan Fenimore Cooper

I never saw a discontented tree. They grip the ground as though they liked it, and though fast rooted they travel about as far as we do.

John Muir

I like trees because they seem
more resigned to the way they
have to live than other things do.

Willa Cather

Though a tree grows so high, the
falling leaves return to the root.

Malay proverb

THOUGHTS & MEMORIES

_____

_____

_____

_____

_____

_____

_____

_____

_____

_____

_____

_____

_____

_____

_____

_____

_____

Guests

THOUGHTS & MEMORIES

_____

_____

_____

_____

_____

_____

_____

_____

_____

_____

_____

_____

_____

_____

_____

_____

_____

_____

_____

Thoughts & Memories

_____

_____

_____

_____

_____

_____

_____

_____

_____

_____

_____

_____

_____

_____

_____

Guests

THOUGHTS & MEMORIES

_____
_____
_____
_____
_____
_____
_____
_____
_____
_____
_____
_____
_____
_____
_____
_____
_____
_____
_____